Khamoshiyaan Unplugged 2.0

Hues of Emotion

Sanjh Sabharwal

Ukiyoto Publishing

Dedication

Sanjay, my muse in the heavens above, I would like to dedicate my compositions to your love, humour and memory. You were the wind beneath my wings and you instilled in me the confidence to stand up in front of the world. Even though we are miles apart in two different worlds, you continue to inspire, motivate and encourage me through your memories to face every challenge in my life without you. Ours was a romance unwritten and unheard ever before and may it continue to those beautiful memories you have left behind. Loads of love…

Contents

Chapter 1 - अतरंगी यारी

इतने ही करीब थे हमारे आप,

कि खुद नहीं कह सके वो सब आप,

हमने तो सिर्फ़ साथ मांगा था आपका,

वजूद, वसीयत, विरासत ना चाही थी आपकी,

दोस्त ही मान कर कर रहें थे बातें,

आपने तो पल में ही बिखेर दी सब बातें,

बोल देते हमें एक बार ही सही,

कि अब यह दोस्ती मुमकिन नहीं,

कोई नहीं हर दोस्ती की एक उमर होती है,

वक़्त ही हर मर्ज़ की दवा होती है,

ना कोई हमदर्द है ना राहगीर है कोई,

दुनिया तो बस एक अन्देखा ख्वाब है कोई.

Chapter 2 - जिंदगी के रंग

ज़िंदगी के रंग तो अब समझे थे हम,

कहने को दोस्त हैं पर फिर भी अकेले थे हम,

ऐसा क्यों लगता है हमे ही इल्म नहीं अपने वजूद का,

क्यों भरोसा नहीं हर रिश्ते की गहराई और सच्चाई का,

किस ने इख़्तियार दिया तुम्हे हमारी ही बुनियाद हिलाने का,

यां थी ही नहीं कोई बुनियाद हमारी बस यह वहम था,

हम ही नही समझ पाये इस आँधी को,

शायद कुछ कमी थी हमारी ही नासमझी को,

करने बैठें हैं अपने वजूद और बुनियाद का ही मंथन,

क्या यही था सच जिसके लिय किया था हमने यह मंथन,

दिल-ओ-दिमाग पर क्यों एक कोहरा सा छाया है,

क्यों हर तरफ एक अजीब सी खामोशी का साया है,

किस कदर बिखर कर रह गयी है अब यह ज़िंदगी,

तुम्हारे बिना बेरंग और बेमानी सी है यह ज़िंदगी l

Chapter 3 - Mothers

Mothers are a blessing in disguise,

God's poised & graceful presence in a guise,

Leading her children to reach greater and unheard-of heights,

Encouraging them to meet challenges without a fright,

Being an epitome of virtue, poise & grace,

Inspiring and motivating to face life without a grimace,

Showing them how to be gentle and soft yet strong,

Instilling in them the confidence to do no wrong,

Cheering them on through each thick and thin,

Nurturing in them to be kind, giving & caring to the brim,

Silently guiding them to love everyone with their hearts,

To never harbour a feeling of hatred in their hearts,

Blessed are those who have this special angel in their lives,

To add love, laughter and happiness to their wonderful lives.

Chapter 4 - आशिकी

वो कहते हैं हम उनका दिल और आशिकी हैं,

पर क्या करें अपने दिल का जिसकी धड़कन कोई और है,

लाख कोशिश कर ली कि तुम्हे हम से इश्क़ ना हो,

तुम तो जाने क्या देख कर हम पर फ़िदा हो,

डरते हैं कि कहीं तुमको भी वो ताउम्र का दर्द ना हो,

जो असीम दर्द हमे आज भी है और ताउम्र भी हो ,

लाख कोशिश कर ली समझने की

पर यह परवाना है कि समझता ही नहीं

किसी को इतना इख़्तियार अपनी ज़िंदगी पर मत दीजिये

कि उनके जाने के बाद बस आँसू ही रह जाएँ

हमने भी की थी मोहब्बत टूट कर किसी से

उनके जाने के बाद खुद ही टूट कर रह गए।

Chapter 5-Fleeting Thoughts

Many a times I sit perplexed & tensed,

Many a times I want to sit undisturbed,

Trying to make sense of the world around me,

Such cold heartedness is the real truth & reality,

We no longer show kindness, humility or care,

Self-centred & selfish that we don't want to share,

Between friendship & enmity there is no disparity,

Known & unknown have merged to become a parity

How strange and untrue have the times become,

Isolated and lonely islands we have all now become,

So, what's all the dazzle and glitter that we, see?

Is it just a façade or a mirage for all to, see?

Chapter 6 - Does Time Really Fly?

Does time really fly??

Or is it too difficult to pass by??

A question which hounds any mind,

An answer which we are still unable to find,

Is it just a simple mind set,

Or there are mysteries to it yet,

Life just seems to be flowing at its pace,

We are all travelers each going to a different place,

Then why is that our paths intertwine,

Is there some logic or reason or just a whine,

Undeciphered is our very existence together,

Or is it an undisturbed and unruffled feather,

Lost in these silly fantasies of the mind,

Oblivious of the answers which we would find,

Are heart throbs and heartaches the two sides?

Which in every heart does resides?

From the start to the end of life,

We just move unknowingly facing life's strife.

Chapter 7 - Lost In Time

Lost in the times flying by,

Little realisation of the darkening sky,

Looked up to see a complete aura of dark,

Startles me back to reality in a stark,

Who could have imagined to find comfort and bliss,

In that light hearted chattering without a miss,

Skies turned a sudden shade of grey,

Bringing back the realities of life in the fray,

Sat motionless even in the approaching dark,

Not wanting to lighten with a glowing spark,

No one knows how long one stayed,

Reminiscent of the memories that slayed,

Turbulent thoughts tossed around in the mind,

Creating an uncanny presence of a different kind,

Bells tolling in the distant afar,

Nothing did quell the turbulence created so far,

Putting the heart in a flutter,

Each fleeting moment began to matter,

As dawn would signal the painful end,

Of the saga of a long-lost friend,

In these few and passing measures of time,

Had created a relationship so sublime,

Knowing well that there is no stoppage to the flow of time,

Cherishing those last moments of ecstasy one last time,

Tomorrow will bring in a new milestone its wake,

Unaware of the pain it created in its wake.

Chapter 8 - मेरा ज़िक्र

क्या हर लम्हे में मेरा ज़िक्र रहता है,

हज़ार रँगों में तुम्हे बैरंग पसंद है l

मैं तो यूँही तुम्हे दीवाना कहती रहती हूँ,

मैं तो अभी भी उसकी यादों में खोयी हूँ,

और शायद मुझ से बड़ा दीवाना और कोई नहीं,

मैं तो अभी भी उसकी यादों में खोयी हूँ कहीं l

Chapter 9 - Friendship

I know our friendship had a rocky start,

You were not too keen to be friends from the start,

Unsure, perturbed and distrustful were you,

Why did I want your friendship you had no clue,

If you ask me even, I didn't quite understand it too,

With the passage of time our friendship just grew,

Today you are one the best people I have in life,

Supporting me through every challenge & life's strife,

In return I can only really wish for you & say,

May all the good things you wish for come your way,

Blessings of young & old be showered upon you,

Our friendship till the end of time, may it continue.

Chapter 10 - Wavering Mind

The mind is a wavering and fleeting cloud,

Where dreams & aspirations often crowd,

Worries & uncertainties forever cloud this frail mind

Rooting doubt & insecurity amongst others of this kind,

Yet to meet challenges head on without a fright,

Not to give up without a shot or valiant fight,

Isn't it the unseen strength of the same frail mind?

Puzzling & intriguing are the mysteries of this frail mind,

Understanding of which, we are yet to unravel & find,

Mindset is all what the mind is trying to remind??

Till we really fathom the real connotations and interpretations of our mind,

Continue to be baffled by manifestations of our imaginative mind!!

Chapter 11 - बेरुखी

जाने इतनी भी क्या बेरूखी थी,

हमसे अब बातें भी नहीं करनी थी,

याॅं फिर सच में कुछ हमसे ही खता हुई,

याँ फिर हम पर ही उन्हें ऐतबार नहीं,

शायद हमने ही इतने इम्तिहाँ लिए सब्र के,

कि टूट गये बाँध हौसले और उनके सब्र के,

हम भी क्या करें इस दीवाने दिल का,

जो बैठा है अपने ही अतीत में तब का।

Chapter 12 - नई सुबह

हर सुबह एक नयी रणभूमि होती है समक्ष,

ले कर नए पहलू , उलझने, पड़ाव और प्रत्यक्ष,

ज़हनसीब हमारे जो हम किसी के ज़हन में शामिल,

वरना हमें तो अच्छा ही लगता है वो माहौल बिन महफ़िल

जहाँ कोई ना हो हमसे सवाल जवाब करने के लिए,

घंटों बैठ सकते हैं अपने ख़यालों में बिन एक साँस लिए।

Chapter 13 - Creativity

Creativity: what is it, I often wonder...

Hours, days, weeks & years go by in ponder...

Are you the music that flows from the soul and soothes the heart?

Are you that mad dream which wakes me with a start?

Are you those words which escape from the thin black shiny pen??

Are you those hues of colour which create a feeling of Zen??

Are you those flowing silhouettes of satin & silk??

Are you those tantalising and creamy desserts of milk??

Are you the soft, gentle and serene touches of nature at play??

Are you the excitement and thrill of the cricket match in play??

Are you the sadness that reverberates with each & every heavenly depart??

Are you the remembrance of the warm hug or the light kiss of the timeless romance??

The list runs endless as the manifold experiences & choices.

The limitless expressions & articulations of the innumerable voices.

Chapter 14 - Love

What is love??

Love is...

A song that escapes the yearning heart,

A poem that expresses the beauty of the soul,

A story that creates a fleeting yet reminiscent impression,

A painting that mesmerizes and captures the inner being.

Chapter 15 - दिल क्या है ?

दिल क्या है?

एक नग़मा है जो हर छोटा बड़ा दिल गाता है,

एक रंग है जो हर बाहार में नज़र आता है,

एक पहेली है जो हर शख़्स को अपने में उलझाती है,

एक एहसास है जो बिन कहे सब कुछ कह जाता है.

Chapter 16 – Silent Clamour

As thoughts and ideas converge on what to write,

Instantaneously am reminded of nature's unfathomed plight,

How has it been so far ravaged & plundered to the very soul?

Unmindful and insensitive to the repercussions for our own very soul,

Bridled with unthinkable traumas, injuries & hurt manifold,

Unimaginable is the devastation unleashed so far unheard & untold,

The times when nature used to soothe every aching heart,

For all that we have done is to shred the very fabric apart,

So much so that our very existence is now in question,

Can we stem the looming & impending annihilation?

Chapter 17 - नई शायरी

लेकर बैठे थे हाथों में नई कलम हम,

सोचा था कुछ नया लिखेंगें आज हम,

उलझ कर रह गए बस अपने ख्यालों में हम,

दिल ने कहा आ लौट चलें उन राहों पर फिर हम,

यादों के करवानं में अक्सर गुम हो जाते हैं हम,

उन हसीं पलों को याद करके फिर मुस्कुराह लेते हैं हम.

Chapter 18 - Fleeting Thoughts

Lost in the hurtling times flying fleetingly by,

Thoughts seem to be changing in each flicker of the eye,

Seemingly like a never ceasing whirlwind all the time,

Reflective of ages traversed through the moments in time,

With intermittent seconds of lull in these tribulations,

Wondering about these unexplained manifestations,

Do any scientific or logical explanations for these really exist?

Or some inexplicable and transcendental phenomenon does exist?

Chapter 19 - To Be Or Not To Be

To be or not to be is always going to be question to see,

So fickle-minded that beyond ourselves we fail to see,

How have we seen such a drastic transformation?

Lost ourselves in this race of fallacy & exaggeration,

Fallen to the intoxications of narcissism & self-promotion,

Ignoring the plight of the helpless & underprivileged in these commotions,

Reminiscing of those days gone by & golden yesteryears,

Where mankind supported each & every one of their peers,

Brings to mind a reality so unreal, harsh & tough,

Is the human being, being human enough??

Chapter 20 - लम्हा लम्हा

क्या लम्हा ही अब सब कुछ है??

मोहब्बत भी एक लम्हा ही तो है,

और रंझ भी एक लम्हा ही सही,

क्या लम्हे की अहमियत इतनी सी ही,

और जो लम्हा अब है ही नहीं,

क्या उसका कोई वजूद ही नहीं,

लम्हों में उलझ कर रह गयी बस ज़िंदगी,

क्या यही है मोहब्बत की इबादत और बन्दगी,

क्यूँ कभी पहले ना समझे हम लम्हों को,

समैट लें यां फिर जाने दें बीते लम्हों को??

वो कहते हैं ज़िंदगी है बस लम्हा भर,

हर उस लम्हे पर यकीन और ऐतबार कर,

जी ले हर उस लम्हे को जी भर,

ज़िंदगी तो साँझ है बस लम्हा भर.

Chapter 21 - Silence

The most difficult & expensive is the silence of the mind,

The cheapest & easiest is the clamour of power & ego intertwined,

For now, let's contemplate the silence of the guns,

Where destruction is manifold and by the tonnes,

Yet again we have proved that we can be fooled & misled,

Through meaningless & manipulative garble of a so-called friend,

Who has but to face all the hurt & brunt of an escalation,

None other than the one who gave into this unseen instigation.

Chapter 22 - अनकहे एहसास

बीते कुछ दिनों में ऐसा क्यूँ लगता है,

कुछ खफा हैं यां सिर्फ़ मेरा वहम है,

जितना भी मैं समझने की कोशिश मे रहूँ,

फिर भी समझ नहीं आता कि क्या पूछूँ यां कहूँ,

कि मुझ से ऐसी क्या कोई खता हुई,

कि दरमियाँ हमारे ये अंजान दूरियाँ हुई,

बस इन्ही ख्यालों में बीत जाती है यह रैना,

बहुत कुछ शायद है मुझे तुमसे आज भी है कहना,

फर्क सिर्फ़ अपने इस हसीन सफर का यह है,

कुछ अनकहे और अनसुने एहसासों का सफर यह है.

Chapter 23 - Fading Romance

It seemed a romantic love story not so long ago,

With each passing day his fondness seems to grow,

Those initial days of wooing her at each & every pretext,

She understood each & every emotion & context

Yet ignorance she feigned just not to encourage

Relentless in his attempt he failed to be discouraged,

Shaking her head at the couplets that he would send,

Encouraging him to document his poems till the end,

Even now their light-hearted bantering and teasing continues to echo,

The tinkling laughter & the purity of love would now cease to echo.

Chapter 24 - फुर्सत के दो पल

वो कहते हैं कि उनके हर ख्याल मे हम हैं,

वो कहते हैं कि उनकी हर साँस मे हम हैं,

वो कहते हैं कि उनका वजूद ही हम हैं,

मगर ना जाने कुछ दिनों से वो ही कहाँ गुम हैं??

इतना भी अपने काम की उलझनों मे मत खो जाईये,

फुरसत के कुछ पल मिलें तो हमें ही वहाँ ना पाईये,

मुक्कमल जहाँ नहीं मिलता है हर किसी को,

नही मिलता यहाँ प्यार ज़िंदगी में हर किसी को.

Chapter 25 - फासले

बहुत से अनकहे और अनसुने फासले हैं दरमियाँ,

हर अल्फ़ाज़ समटे था लफ्ज़ों की ज़ुबाँ अपने दरमियाँ,

जाने किस मोड़ पर बिछड़ गए थे दो हमसफर,

रास्ते ही बदल गए थे शायद अब जीवन भर,

जैसे टूटता है फ़लक से कोई हसीन दिलकश सितारा,

अनसुना और अनकहा रह गया बहुत कुछ मेरे यारा.

Chapter 26 - A Giant Merry Go Round

The World's but a giant merry go round,

Inexplicable mysteries which continue to astound,

Unfettered emotions & sentiments hovering around,

Heart aches & heart breaks continue to surround

Leaving many of us utterly confused and spell bound

Is it the real truth or hazy imagination profound??

Chapter 27 - Expressions Unsaid

Some unsaid words linger on... yours & mine,

Some unheard expressions linger on... yours & mine,

Some hidden pain lingers on... yours & mine,

Some touching emotions & feelings linger on... yours & mine.

Chapter 28 - Unexplained Emotions

Are you there in all my memories or are my memories because of you??

Are you there in all my thoughts or are my thoughts because of you??

Are you there in all my words or are my words because of you??

My heart keeps beating or is my heartbeat because of you??

At least tell me that you are my life or is my life because of you??

Chapter 29 - Forever Love

I promise to you today my love to tell me:

What will it cost to bring that wonderful smile to your beautiful face??

If I can't bring that smile then what is my love for??

How can you smile for the world when you feel like crying inwardly??

If I can't bring that peace to your heart, then what is my love for??

All your worries and fears that you hold so closely to your heart,

If I can't become your confidante, then what is my love for??

How you manage the art of being alone in a social gathering??

If I can't become your partner in life, what is my love for??

Chapter 30 - वक़्त

क्या वक़्त और उसके मिज़ाज़ में उलझ कर रह गए आप,

हमने तो यूँ ही लम्हों का ज़िक्र किया था चुप चाप,

यूँ ही अल्फ़ाज़ों को पीरोया था हमने एक आम जुमले में,

और आपने उसे हकीकत मान लिया एक ही पल में,

लफ्ज़ों का यही है अतरंगी रंग और रूप,

कभी घनी छाँव तो कभी किलकिलाती धूप.

Chapter 31 - Morning Musings

Sipping warm coffee every morning I let the mind wander,

Upon the actions & reactions of the mind I do ponder,

Where are we all in some hurry and worry to go,

For all that meets the eye is the scurry & flurry on the go,

Can't we just take a deep breath and a break,

Forgetting the tribulations and clamouring in its wake,

Let's soak up the tranquillity of nature around us,

And not try to behave as if we were on the last bus,

Life has so much more and plenty to offer to us all,

If we could just step back from the haste of it all.

Chapter 32 - पलटते पन्ने

यूँही बैठे थे हम जीवन के पन्ने पलटते हुए,

कि फिर कुछ छू सा गया यूँही गुज़रते हुए,

कभी सोचा ना था कि एक पड़ाव यह भी आएगा,

कि ज़िंदगी का हर एक पहलू धूंधला नज़र आएगा,

हम फिर से मजबूर हुए सोचने के लिए,

सब एक भ्रम था और लब थे हमने सी लिए,

क्यूँ रंजहोगम की सियाही थी फैली हुई हर दिशा में,

यां फिर कोई खता ही थी हमारी ही समझ में.

Chapter 33 - ख्वाब याँ हकीकत

ख्वाब है याँ कोई हकीकत यह ना समझ पाये हम,

हर पहर यूँही सोचने पर मज़बूर हुए हम,

क्यूँ यूँ अंजान बना बैठा था इंसान,

क्यूँ एक हैवान बन बैठा था इंसान,

ना कोई दर्द छूता था इसे अब कभी,

ना बढ़ाता था यह हाथ मदद में कभी,

क्या यह कुदरत का कोई अजीब सा नया खेल था,

यां यूँही बेखबर और बेदर्द बन बैठा था,

इसी उलझन में घँटों निकल जाते थे,

और एहसास थे की पुरानी राहों पर निकल जाते थे,

जहाँ से लौटने का सोचने से ही कतराते थे हम,

यह किस वीराने में आ कर थम गए थे कदम,

दिल ने दी फिर एक दस्तक और हमसे कहने लगा,

कि और अब ना दे अपने दिल को यह बेमतलब की दगा,

और लौट चल अपने हसींन और खूबसूरत कल में,

जहाँ हर चेहरा बिखेरता था एक मुस्कुराहट एक ही पल में

Chapter 34 - Forgotten Love

That tinkling laughter which made him smile,

Egging him on through the toughest mile,

Always by his side through rain and snow,

Little did he realise or would ever know,

That for whom he held so much love & compassion,

Never meant to reciprocate the same passion,

For her heart was claimed and lost long ago,

To a knight valiant and handsome long ago,

So much so that even in the modern day,

You wouldn't find such a love today,

Even though he no longer is alive or around,

Yet it is by those memories that she waits on the ground,

Wishing & praying for her long lost heart,

Yearning to no longer remain poles apart,

But I guess she has a journey of her own,

Lament she doesn't and neither does she moan,

Finding his presence in all things bright & beautiful,

She creates newer designs so inspiring & beautiful.

Chapter 35 - Fallacy Of Time

Is time really what we think it is??

Or just an inconclusive reality it is??

Thoughts zip through this slumbering mind,

Or is it a trance of an unimaginable kind??

It seems like a repetitive & never ending déja vu deadlock,

Leaving the person confused, unnerved and taking stock,

Putting up the need to question the heart's desire,

Was there anything in the heart that kindles a fire??

None can ever touch a broken, aching & shattered heart,

Nothing could ever have the healing touch to soothe the heart.

Chapter 36 - कहानी

हर नया दिन लाता है अपने संग एक नयी कहानी,

बयां करती है एक नए लम्हे और एहसास को ज़ुबानी,

कुछ मीठे और कुछ खट्टे एहसासों की बनती है यह कहानी,

समेंटे हुये हज़ारों बातें अपने अंदर है यह कहानी,

कुछ कही तो कुछ अनकही,

कुछ सुनी तो कुछ अनसुनी,

कुछ सच्ची तो कुछ रूहानी,

इतनी सी है हर नए दिन की यह कहानी.

Chapter 37 - वजूद

अक्सर हम सोचा करते हैं

जिंदगी का क्या वजूद है

की पल में ही यह बदल जाती है

यूँही चलते चलते, राह बदल जाती है

और नए मोड़ और पड़ाव सामने आते हैं

उलझा जाती है और सोचने पर मज़बूर करती है

कि क्या इतना ही वजूद इसका है

यां और भी पहलु इसके समझने को हैं

बिखेर कर रख देती हमारे विश्वास को यह है

जिंदगी एक विचित्र पहेली है

जिसे सुलझाना अभी बाकी है

कहाँ से शुरू और कहाँ खत्म होती है

अंसुल्झी सी पहेली यह है.

Chapter 38 - आंसू

आँसू भी कितने अजीब हैं

खुशी हो तो यह यूँही बहते हैं

गम हो तो इनका बहना लाज़मी है

और कई बार तो यह बिन वजह ही बहते हैं

अब यह कैसे पता चले कि इंसान खुशी में बहा रहा है

यां कोई गम है जिसे बता रहा है

वाह रे आँसु तेरी भी अजीब ही दास्ताँ है ।

Chapter 39 - दिल का फितूर

कैसा है यह फितूर दिल का,

यां यह असर है इस मौसम का,

आस पास सितम ढाह रही हो कायनात,

गर सिर्फ आशिकी रहती है कम्बख्त दिल को याद ,

अजीब दस्तूर यह जो मोहब्बत है,

किसी और के लिए खुद को दीवाना बना देती है,

ना वक़्त का इल्म ना ज़माने का डर

बन कर दीवाना फिरते हैं मेहबूब दर-ब-दर,

क्या अंजाम हो आशिकी का यह भी इल्म नहीं

गर फिर भी दीवाने को कम इश्क़ नहीं.

Chapter 40 - Words

Words, words, words & even more words,

Have the power to ruffle the strongest of chords,

Touches hues of emotion to the very core,

Stories and anecdotes just seem to outpour,

Reminiscent of experiences, instances never told,

Magical moments unravelled or foretold,

How they cast a spell so mesmerising,

Lost in imagination so vivid and uncompromising,

At times the heart skips a beat or two,

Is it an unfathomed reality so true?

All we attribute to it is just mere words,

Will we ever value the power of these words?

Chapter 41 - Emojis

Perspectives, interpretations & expressions galore,

Meanings, emotions & pining and much more,

Where the length, breadth and depth of words ends,

Arrives a language which creates new trends,

Born from the noiseless chatter of technology,

Is a nouveau world of Emoji,

A caress so gentle & feather-light,

Transforms into an ecstasy so bright,

Unfolding a world intriguing and new,

Puzzling, confusing and at times bewildering too.

Chapter 42 - ख़्वाब

ख़्वाब ही तो है ज़िंदगी और क्या है,

अनकहे एहसास और हसरतें ही तो हैं,

हर दिल में दबी हुई वो अनकही आरज़ू ही तो है,

अफसोस की बे लगाम ही तो है,

बदल जाए कब और किस तरफ यह ज़िंदगी,

पहेली ही बन कर रह गयी यह ज़िंदगी,

इसका आरंभ भी एक हसीं करिश्मा है कोई,

इसके अंत के बाद का आरंभ भी एक पहेली है कोई,

जिसे ना कोई जान पाया कोई,

ना ही समझ पाया इसे कोई.

Chapter 43 - What is love?

What is love??

Is it the gentle touch of a lover's hand??

Is it the snuggling of a baby with the mother??

Is it the unrelenting chattering of the birds??

Is it the caress of the breeze on the cheek??

Is it the lull after the parting of a loved one??

Is it the tinkling of a wind chime??

Is it the sweet fragrance of the wet earth??

Is it the fluttering of one's heart in anticipation??

Or is it all of the above and much more.

Chapter 44 - हर एक Friend ज़रूरी होता है

हर एक friend ज़रूरी होता है,

कुछ हँसते हैं संग हमारे,

तो कुछ रोते भी हैं संग हमारे,

ज़िंदगी की इस कश-म-कश में,

हर एक friend ज़रूरी होता है,

कितनी बार साथ छूट जाता है,

कितनी बार अपना कोई रूठ जाता है,

कुछ के संग बीती मीठी बातें,

कुछ के साथ वो तीखे बोल,

हर एक friend ज़रूरी होता है,

कुछ का साथ किसी भी तूफ़ाँ में नही छूटा,

कुछ तो महज़ एक हवा के झोंके से बिखर गए,

हर वो खट्टे मीठे पल हैं याद,

घंटों बेफ़िज़ूल बातों में उलझे रहना,

हर एक friend ज़रूरी होता है,

काश के वो वक़्त फिर से ठहर जाता,

जी लें फिर से वो बचपन के बेफिक्र दिन,

गुज़र जाएँ फ़िर उन अंसुलझी राहों से

क्योंकि हर एक friend ज़रूरी होता है

Chapter 45 - Smiles

Smiles spread so much light,

Making the heart swell with delight,

All it needs is a curve of the lips,

Infectious & contagious-everyone it grips,

From tiny toddlers to the vintage & classic kind,

Almost all you know and can find,

It takes just a curve & a while,

To break into the super sensational smile,

It's the only known curve to set things straight,

From a forgotten birthday to being late for a date,

Precious & expensive gift for all mankind,

Is the smile so simple and undefined?

Chapter 46 - ख्वाइशें

ख्वाइशें कितनी अंजान और बिन पहचान,

कैसी हैं यह बिन किसी अक्स के और बेजान,

फिर भी छू लेतीं हैं हर दिल-ओ-दिमाग़ को

क्या प्रतिबिंब है जो घेर लेता है हर इंसान को,

यां फिर बेरंग सा कोई अंदेखा अरमान हो,

सोचने पर मजबूर कर दे हर इंसान को,

कैसा इसका यह अजब रूप है,

हर जगह हर लम्हा जीत जो लेता है,

बिन किसी बल, बिन किसी छल के,

दुनिया कायल हो जाती पल मे,

वाह री ख्वाइश, विचित्र ही है तेरी कहानी,

कितने हैं रंग और रूप कह   सके नही जुबानी.

Chapter 47 - Beauty

Beauty lies in the eyes of the beholder,

Ages past this has stuck in our minds akin to a boulder,

Can it be defined as so actually?

Can it be defined so in reality?

Is it that captivating smile on a tired face??

Is it the tear in the eye of a joyful face?

Is it those stealthy and pining glances of the first crush??

Is it those angry looks of a lifelong love in anguish??

Is it the undefined victory of a long-lost warrior in battle??

Is the death knell resounding at the end of battle??

Is it that forgotten & soothing symphony of an era gone by??

Is the cacophony of the unrelenting clamor nearby??

Is it the lull before that inexplicable storm in life??

Is it silent frenzy & crescendo that marks the end of life??

Chapter 48 - Happiness

Happiness is...

the gentle breeze blowing through a lover's hair,

the excitement of seeing your favourite star live,

the roaring laughter after playing a successful prank,

the strong cup of coffee with a best friend,

the joy of driving your mean machine for the first time,

the sharing of that sizzling brownie with your sibling,

the thundering clapping for a friend on winning a boxing bout,

the getting wet in the rain while sharing the umbrella,

the long phone calls of lovers spanning the night,

the never-ending argument over where to sit in class,

the short-lived joy of school vacations,

the travelling on the footstep of an overcrowded bus,

the senseless rambling when you meet your first crush,

the rolling over in the grass after a day's fun,

the hanging of heads when we are caught in the act,

the restful sleep knowing that your best friend is there,

And much much more...

Chapter 49 - ज़िंदगी

इबादत क्या है?

बंदगी क्या है?

 ज़िंदगी क्या है?

ख्वाब है यां हक़ीक़त है?

इसी सवाल में उलझ के रह जाते हैं कि इबादत क्या है,

ता उम्र बीत जाती है समझने में बंदगी क्या है,

और जब तक समझ आता है कि ज़िंदगी क्या है,

साँसें ही साथ देती नही तो क्या समझें कि यह सब क्या है.

Chapter 50 - इंतज़ार

समय के इंतज़ार मे जीवन ही खत्म हो जाता है,

दिल की चाहतें और अरमाँ दिल में ही रह जाता है,

वक़्त का क्या इंतज़ार और क्या ऐतबार,

यह कब किसी का हुआ है जो हम करें इस पर ऐतबार,

यह तो रेत की तरह यूँही फिसल जाता है,

और फिर इंसान अफसोस करता रह जाता है,

वक़्त का क्यूँ इतना इंतज़ार करना है,

आगे बढ़ और इसे खुद ही हासिल करना है,

क्योंकि वक़्त किसी का आता नही,

जो वक़्त को जीत सके वो किसी का वजूद और फ़ितरत नही .

Chapter 51 - Undying Love

You are there in every breath that I take,

You are there in every moment that I'm awake,

You are there in every step of my life,

Egging me on through all the strife,

Inspiring & motivating me all the while,

To light up other's lives with my ravishing smile,

You have taught me to take these challenges in my stride,

To stand up tall & hold up my head with immense pride,

At how I have shown unflinching courage & strength in your absence,

Gratitude is all I can express for His & your unwavering presence.

Chapter 52 - बीते लम्हे

तेरे जाने के बाद सब कुछ थम सा गया,

वो शाम जो कभी खुशनुमा थी,

वो आज तेरे इंतज़ार मे बेचैन थी,

लम्हे कब दिन और कब साल बन गए,

लम्हे यूँ ही एक बहता दरिया बन गए,

 मैं और मेरी कॉफी अक्सर यूँही बतिया लेते हैं

अपने दिल की वो धड़कन कॉफी को सुना लेते हैं,

कॉफी भी हंस कर हमसे कह देती है,

कहाँ अतीत में फिर चली तू जाती है,

नये ख्वाब बुन और चल पर उस नई और अंजानी डगर पर,

सूरज भी तो तन्हा है गर रोज़ नई सुबह लाता है मुस्कुरा कर।

Chapter 53 - Demons Of The Mind

Demons of the mind come out to play,

In the dead of the night the mind they slay,

Tossing & turning thoughts follow in the wake,

Relinquishing the peace and keeping me awake,

What are they in reality?

Fragments of memory in virtuality?

Or some latent desire of the heart unfulfilled?

Or an incomprehensible muse of the mind undistilled?

Many an hour I stay up trying to define,

Still remains yet to articulate or define.

Chapter 54 - Clamouring Voices

Voices, voices, and even more voices around me,

Forever chiding, disciplining or deranging my thoughts & me,

Clamouring to reach the inner me with unfailing logic & reason,

Forever trying to drown me with foolishness through every season,

Pegging a square in circle or circle in a square,

Defiant & unruly to earn that discerning stare,

So much so that the only solace that i did find,

Was in the innate creativity of the unrestricted mind,

Unleashed & undisturbed it traversed through all realms of life,

Till it mellowed down to the peace from the unfettered din of life.

Chapter 55 - Spectral Reminiscences

Uncanny sensations & tingling recollections spring up out of the blue,

Unannounced these trigger the turbulences of thoughts out of the blue,

Is it a premonition of ominous messages being foretold??

Is it the spine-chilling intuition of some mishap being foretold??

Thoughts like this creep up every now and then,

Always in times of sadness & shock engulf us when,

Yet this is what happens when we get that dreaded news,

Of a companion whose loving face will no longer be there for views,

Left numb and confused at this shattering and heart-breaking news,

Taken back to comprehend & understand this undeciphered muse,

Life is but a mystery which is incomprehensible & unravelled,

If the beginning was marvelling, its end remains unparalleled.

About the Author

Sanjh Sabharwal

Sanjh's extensive experience in diverse academic domains as a teacher, mentor, trainer and global educator cements her as an indispensable part of the Education industry. Her quest for being a lifelong learner and farsightedness during the needs of time make her a great success in her work.

Her passion to stand up to the challenges of different curricula is the hallmark of her versatility as a global educator. She nurtures the quality of empathy to be one among the learners to understand and work on their strengths and weaknesses and her own to ever be an eternal learner.

Her love for language and literature drove her to try her hand in writing by publishing her pioneer bilingual work of poetry "Khamoshiyaan Unplugged" and now "Khamoshiyaan Unplugged 2.0". Besides these two books, she has contributed to the literary pulpit through her poetry, short stories & letters through publication platforms like Story Mirror, Ukiyoto, Blue Rose amongst others.

You can connect with her on her insta page @ sanjh.sabharwal.